I SEE GHOSTS!

LEARN TO CONTROL YOUR PSYCHIC ABILITES THROUGH

DISCIPLINE AND MEDITATION

BY

PAUL G. ROGERS

Copyrighted in March 2015 BY PAUL G. ROGERS

ISBN: 978-1508852902

e-mail: www.paulrogers@pgrparanormal.com

Web site: www.pgrparanormal.com

Cellular number: 626-483-1967

TABLE OF CONTENTS

INTRODUCTION

1. FINDING YOURSELF

2. TYPES OF PSYCHIC ABILITIES

3. THE SEVEN CHAKRAS

4. CONTROLLING THAT VERY BUSY MIND AND MEDITATING

5. NIRVANA

6. BEING IN CONTROL

INTRODUCTION

I have been a Medium and ghost investigator for 11 years now and still thoroughly love doing investigations and readings. My specialty is removing ghosts from homes or businesses, for it gives me great joy to see the owners happy and content because the ghost problem they had is now gone. Ghosts, Shadow ghosts or negative entities. Throughout my experiences I have come across time and again people that do not know the meaning of what a ghost is. They were a real live breathing, feeling person that lived on this Earth, but due to his/her own choices had decided to pursue the bad or negative aspects in their lives, causing great pain or suffering to themselves or other human beings. I am talking about murder, rape, incest, molestation, drug or alcohol abuse, or being just plain mean to others. For all the suffering they have caused, when they suddenly die they realize what terrible lives they lived and decide not to go into

The Light and cross over either because of God's wrath, Hell's fire, purgatory or due to their strong addictions, just refuse to leave. They are destined to wander this Earth looking for a suitable host to attach themselves to, to haunt for an indefinite time. They will cause the living person grief by exacerbating their own addictions, or trigger unpleasant situations within the person's home, causing verbal or physical fights, divorce, alcoholism, drug use, nightmares, night terror's, depression, insomnia and possibly illness. It is hard to get rid of them or get them to move on, either down the street or crossing them over to The Other Side.

Paranormal groups have tried everything to remove the negative entities, like smudging (burning sage and spreading salt), Holy water, prolonged prayer, having priests come over and bless the house, to lighting candles and using witch craft. In my experience none of these work for I have been to many homes where all of this was tried and had failed, the problem just got worse. But, that is not why I am writing this particular book. If you are interested in learning more about removing ghosts or my life's work read my first book 'When Shadows are not Shadows at all' available through my web site www.pgrparanormal.com. This book I am writing is for those adults, teenagers and children alike who have natural psychic abilities but do not know how to control them. I mean people who have experienced psychic abilities in the past and want to re-open up or the people who see ghosts or spirits everywhere and are bothered by them day in and day out and just want them to go away. Imagine waking up in the middle of the night and seeing a ghost standing at the foot of their bed or ghosts everywhere you go. It is scary and disturbing not knowing what to do to stop it. They feel they are going crazy and have explored every avenue they could think of to stop seeing these awful beings and to get some peace of mind. There is a way as I will describe my own technique that I developed and has worked for many people. In the following chapters you will learn to control what you see, feel and hear. Knowledge is the best defense in learning how to control your psychic abilities and energy. I will describe my own experiences with learning how to meditate, controlling my psychic energy, making it as easy as turning a light switch on or off. We will get into Chakra's, meditation exercises, acquiring patience, clearing your mind of useless thoughts, believing in yourself, putting trust in yourself that you can control your abilities and achieving Nirvana. But I will insist right here and now that learning my technique will take a lot of time and effort. I am talking about months to learn how, with weekly practice, then maintaining what you have learned so as not to slip back into old bad habits. It took me a year and a half just to feel comfortable with controlling my Chakra energy fields and believing in myself that I had control of what was happening to me. So if you think you can learn this in a couple of weeks, think again. A lifelong dedication will be needed, because the psychic energy you have will be with you forever, so you will have to control it for just as long.

CHAPTER 1

FINDING YOURSELF

Okay before we get started if you read my first book, 'When Shadows are not Shadows at all', then you know when I write it's like I am speaking directly to you. I find it easier to communicate what I am trying to teach you. Please take my explanations as constructive learning. I am not trying to shove information down your throat, but trying my best to explain my technique's as best as I can. If some of this information does not work for you then try a variation of it. But I feel that following it will produce the best results in helping you to control your energies and abilities.

Finding yourself. No, I don't think you are lost or can't find your way home, but with all of the turmoil you are going through it is best to start at the beginning of when you started feeling or seeing ghosts or spirits. If you have had it all of your life, that is good. You will know if you see, feel and hear ghosts. If it has been a short while, then you should have some idea what you are capable of. Either way I want you to write down exactly what you are experiencing. Like seeing apparitions, hearing voices, smelling something familiar in a place where nobody else smells it, feeling ghosts or spirits walking up behind you, seeing ominous shadows walking past you or just remaining in one place. You need to be sure of these things because when we start shutting your Chakras down, you will have to realize that your abilities will shut down too. But don't worry. This is the first thing you must learn in order to get control.

Like I said, I have been doing this for several years and have met many people who tell me, "I see ghosts or spirits and I don't know how to make it stop." Not only have adults told me this, but young adults and even children. After some family background questioning, usually I find out that some other relative, like Mom, Dad, Aunt or Uncle or distant relative has also had some sort of psychic ability. Yes, it is inherited and does carry over to their siblings. I knew my Mother was psychic for a long time, but I just found out four years ago that my Great Aunt used to hold séances, readings and healings for people. I remember as a child when I was sick she would say a prayer in Spanish (yes, I am Hispanic from my Mother's side) to me and take her hands, stroke my face and move her hands away from me while flicking her fingers. Like she was grabbing the germs and flicking them away from me. My Uncle Juan was very psychic, but in a different way. He would communicate with spirit Doctors by thinking of a question on how to heal a particular person, go to sleep and wake up with the answer. So it was passed down from my Mother's side to me.

People with psychic abilities can be scared to even know they have them, denying them every time they experience them. During child hood we all grow up listening to our parents. If we tell them we have a special 'friend' and talk and play with them, they tell us how good it is to have an invisible friend, when In fact it is actually a ghost they are seeing and communicating with. Later when material things, like TV, video games, toys and just life starts getting in the way, they turn off their abilities by ignoring them and put them aside. But inevitably these abilities will come back. Usually after we turn 18 or older they will 'pop' up. That's when it becomes uncomfortable, unbearable or just plain annoying.

There are also the children that never lose their abilities and right through childhood and the teenage years into adult hood they see ghosts or spirits. But it is a lonely existence for they can never talk to friends or their parents about it because they will think they are crazy. When I was young I was not able to see them, just felt them walk up behind me, which to this day they still do. It would cause me to turn around quick thinking someone was following me. Being under 10 years old it was pretty scary. Now I know if they come up behind me they are a ghost. Spirits who have crossed over have the ability to come and go from Heaven quite easily and will approach me from the front. Cowardly ghosts will sneak up behind, which I will turn around, confront and respond one of my Angels to dispatch them to The Holding area where they can never come back. I describe this in my first book.

CHAPTER 2

TYPES OF PSYCHIC ABILITIES

Here are some explanations about different psychic abilities. Some psychics have one, two or all of these abilities. I am able to see, hear, feel, smell and touch objects or pictures and get a reading from them.

Clairvoyance

The term **clairvoyance** (from French *clair* meaning "clear" and *voyance* meaning "vision") is used to refer to the ability to gain information about an object, person, location or physical event through means other than the known senses, i.e., a form of extra-sensory perception. A person said to have the ability of clairvoyance is referred to as a **clairvoyant** ("one who sees clearly").

Clairsentience (feeling/touching)

In the field of parapsychology, **clairsentience** is a form of extra-sensory perception wherein a person acquires psychic knowledge primarily by feeling. The word "clair" is French for "clear", and "sentience" is derived from the Latin sentire, "to feel". Psychometry is related to clairsentience. The word stems from *psyche* and *metric*, which means "soul-measuring".

Clairaudience (hearing/listening)

In the field of parapsychology, **clairaudience** [from late 17th century French *clair* (clear) and audience (hearing)] is a form of extra-sensory perception wherein a person acquires information by paranormal auditory means. It is often considered to be a form of clairvoyance. Clairaudience is essentially the ability to hear in a paranormal manner, as opposed to paranormal seeing (clairvoyance) and feeling (clairsentience).

Clairalience (smelling)

Also known as **clairescence.** In the field of parapsychology, **clairalience** (or alternatively, **clairolfactance**) [presumably from late 17th century French *clair* (clear) and alience (smelling)] is a form of extra-sensory perception wherein a person accesses psychic knowledge through the physical sense of smell.

Claircognizance (knowing)

In the field of parapsychology, **claircognizance** [presumably from late 17th century French *clair* (clear) and *cognizance* (<ME*cognisaunce* < Ofr *conoissance*, knowledge)] is a form of extra-sensory perception wherein a person acquires psychic knowledge primarily by means of intrinsic knowledge. It is the ability to know something without a physical explanation why you know it, like the concept of Mediums.

Clairgustance (tasting)

In the field of parapsychology, **clairgustance** is defined as a form of extra-sensory perception that allegedly allows one to taste a substance without putting anything in one's mouth. It is claimed that those who possess this ability are able to perceive the essence of a substance from the spiritual or ethereal realms through taste.

Try and figure out which one(s) closely describes what you are experiencing. When you do, pick the one that is the strongest and later we will concentrate on that.

Mediumship is the practice of certain people—known as mediums—to purportedly mediate communication between spirits of the dead and living human beings.[1][2]

CHAPTER 3

THE SEVEN CHAKRAS

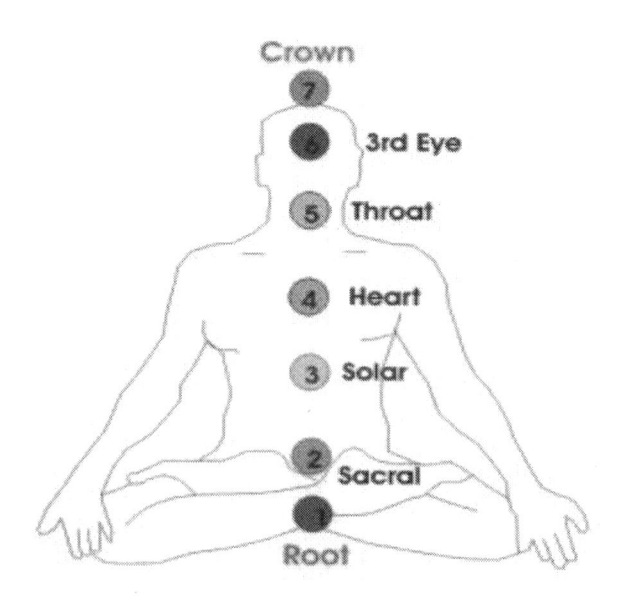

Chakra 1 - the Base (or Root Chakra)

Its color is red and it is located at the perineum, base of your spine. It is the Chakra closest to the earth. Its function is concerned with earthly grounding and physical survival. This Chakra is associated with your legs, feet, bones, large intestine and adrenal glands. It controls your fight or flight response. Blockage may manifest as paranoia, fear, procrastination and defensiveness.

Chakra 2 – The Sacral (or Navel Chakra)

Its color is orange and it is located between the base of your spine and your navel. It is associated with your lower abdomen, kidneys, bladder, circulatory system and your reproductive organs and glands. It is concerned with emotion. Blockage may manifest as emotional problems, compulsive or obsessive behavior and guilt.

Chakra 3 – The Solar Plexus

Its color is yellow and is located a few inches above the navel in the solar plexus area. This chakra is concerned with your digestive system, muscles, pancreas and adrenals. It is the seat of your emotional life. Feelings of personal power, laughter, joy and anger are associated with this center. Your sensitivity, ambition and ability to achieve are stored here. Blockage may manifest as anger, frustration, and lack of direction.

Chakra 4 – The Heart

Its color is green and it is located within your heart. It is the center of love, compassion, harmony and peace. The Asians say that this is the house of the soul. This Chakra is associated with your lungs, heart, arms, hands and thymus gland. We fall in love through our heart Chakra, then that feeling of unconditional love moves to the emotional center commonly known as the solar plexus. After that it moves into the Base Chakra where strong feelings of attraction can be released. Blockage can show itself in the immune system, lung and heart problems, or manifest as lack of compassion or unprincipled behavior.

Chakra 5. The Throat

Its color is blue or turquoise and is located within the throat. It is the Chakra of communication, creativity, self-expression and judgment. It is associated with your neck, shoulders, arms, hands, thyroid and parathyroid glands. It is concerned with the senses of inner and outer hearing, the synthesizing of ideas, healing, transformation and purification. Blockage can show up as creative blocks, dishonesty or general problems in communicating ones needs to others.

Chakra 6 – The Third Eye (or Brow Chakra)

Its color is Indigo (a combination of red and blue). It is located at the center of your forehead at eye level or slightly above. This Chakra is used to question the spiritual nature of our life. It is the Chakra of question, perception and knowing. It is concerned with inner vision, intuition and wisdom. Your dreams for this life and recollections of other lifetimes are held in this Chakra. Blockage may manifest as problems like lack of foresight, mental rigidity, 'selective' memory, psychic abilities and depression.

Chakra 7 – The Crown

Its color is violet and is located at the top of your head. It is associate with the cerebral cortex, central nervous system and the pituitary gland. It is concerned with information, understanding, acceptance and bliss. It is said to be your own place of connection to God, the Chakra of Divine purpose and personal destiny. Blockage can manifest as psychological problems.

Please read all of these carefully. These are the things that you will need to know when you are in a meditative state and are trying to control your abilities.

CHAPTER 4

CONTROLLING THAT VERY BUSY MIND AND MEDITATING

Childhood, bills, money problems, relationships, children, relatives, illnesses, your job and just life in general clouds our minds every day. Thoughts that just 'pop' in and out without a care and with lightning speed. We all have them, some more than others. But in today's society we have made ourselves so complicated and busy it even affects our own personal wellbeing, sleep and emotional state. Staying busy is our way of life now and if we have some extra time where we are not doing anything, we will seek out and find something to do just to fill the time. Days go by quickly and you realize all that you had to do today must now spill over into the next day and the next in order to complete all tasks. It is a habit that has formed us into being the person we are and perhaps do not want to be.

WAIT A MINUTE! Take a step back. Do we REALLY need to be SO busy taking care of various mundane things just to feel important with all that we do? NO! We all need to take the time to relax and make time for ourselves. We all need to figure out what's most important in our lives and concentrate on that. In 2003 I had a triple coronary artery heart bypass. It scared the SHIT out of me! As I was lying in my hospital bed and later at home, I realized that there were major things I needed to change. I did a 180 degree turn around in my life, starting with myself and what was important to me, which was me. In February 2004 my Angel John came to me and told me about my abilities that were now going to start coming through and I had to start studying and practicing how to use them. Guess what I had to do to develop my abilities? Your right, meditation. My spirit guide Thomas sent me spirits to help me, as well as I read books and used the internet to read up as much as I could about the subject. If you want to know about Angels or spirit guides please read my first book. Then came the hard part. Actually sitting down and doing it. When I started, it was extremely hard clearing my mind of thoughts that came racing in and out. A lot of stuff that either I had to take care of today or tomorrow. All of the above mentioned problems would creep in too. But I knew I had to clear my mind in order for this to work. So I kept at it for weeks until I felt I had achieved my goal of a clear mind. It took me a year and a half to finally feel comfortable with my meditation skills. I had also been practicing opening and closing my Chakra's, which gave me the control I needed to handle my abilities. Now I can turn my abilities on and off like a light switch and clear my mind in a matter of seconds. How did I do it? Let me tell you how. Of course if you don't like the way I do it, you can pick and choose what works for you.

1. I like a quiet and still room. Some people like to have soothing music on. I have back problems so sitting on the floor with my legs crossed does not work for me, so I sit in a comfortable chair with my feet flat on the floor. You can also do the following technique sitting cross legged on the floor. Next I keep my arms on the arm rests and close my eyes and imagine a large blank screen, like in a movie theater the large white screen you see before the movie starts. Concentrate on that and if a thought pops in tell yourself you will take care of it later and push it out of your mind. Take at least 10 minutes practicing this at least twice a week. When you get comfortable with it, then increase it to 15, 20 or even 30 minutes, three or four times a week. But take your time doing this. Don't rush it. Remember you HAVE to make time

for this. At first you will be frustrated and want to quit. But you have to realize you have been thinking about things to do all of your life and now you are trying to change it. Like working out a muscle, you need to work at it to get better at it. Please have the courage and patience to continue on.

2. Hopefully in one month you will have succeeded in controlling some of your thoughts and have started clearing your mind. This is when you need to start visualizing an energy beam coming from the soles of your feet and projecting it downward telling it mentally to ground your energy with Mother Earth. By connecting your energy to the Earth, you are enabling yourself to control your energies by grounding yourself. Just like electricity needs to be grounded to work, so

does your spiritual energy. You may not believe this or not but it will help when you start opening and closing your Chakra's. Besides what can you lose by doing it?

3. After a couple of weeks of meditating, you should be ready to visually think of a serene scene that will help you feel relaxed. I love the mountains. The wind blowing through the trees, the smell of pine and the crisp air. I visualize sitting in the mountains surrounded by pine trees and a running brook in front of me. It is the calmest place I know of. But as I have said before, you can think of any other place that makes you feel relaxed then do it. Concentrate on the wind blowing through the trees, smells and sound of the water as it flows over the rocks.

Being relaxed and in a calm state of mind is our goal.

4. Have patience! Like I said in the beginning, this is not something you will learn quickly and put to use quickly. It is a life time commitment to your own well-being, controlling your psychic abilities. The main reason to control your abilities now, is so in the future when you get older it will be easier to control them, as in turning them on or off like a light switch.

5. After three months of practicing your meditation, your routine should be pretty well set. You should be able to get yourself into a meditative state quite easily and put yourself into a calm state of mind. The time you spend meditating should not be more than 30 minutes. That's all I like to do. Any longer and I come out of it feeling

sleepy and tired. Meditation is supposed to make you feel good, mentally and physically. Now is the time to start opening and closing your Chakra energy points. What I do is focus my mind on the root Chakra, then work my way up. I concentrate on the spot and relax my mind and visualize the Chakra spot opening up like a door and a beam of light or energy emitting from it. Hold the outgoing light for a few seconds, then visualize the door closing. Do this for all of your Chakras. By performing this regularly and every time you meditate, this will give you the control you need to ensure you don't see or hear ghosts unless you want to. You see the ghosts are attracted to your life energy and like the feeling of it. By closing your energy points, it will prevent them from coming around, no matter where you are.

6. After practicing opening and closing your Chakra's for another month, if you feel comfortable and are ready to go to the next step I want you to start opening and closing your 3rd Chakra, where your psychic energy is the strongest, when you are out and about running errands, like at the grocery store, at work or even when doing chores at home. Just stop and visualize the 3rd Chakra door opening up and then closing. Getting used to this is very important, for no matter where you go you will be running into ghosts or spirits. Once you get used to doing this, try visually in your mind expanding your energy outward, more and more each time until the energy fills the room. This

technique is what you will use to open up and see the ghost's physical characteristics. You can also use the 6th Chakra to see ghosts and spirits as well. Personally I use both because I have been doing this for so long it is second nature to me. **But always remember to shut it down.** You don't want to leave your energy open and have an unwanted guest attach themselves to you and bring it home.

7. One more thing I want to mention. If you are not interested in seeing spirits or ghosts, then follow the above techniques and close your Chakras permanently. I would still meditate occasionally to make sure the Chakras are closed, because in my experience sometimes they will just open up on their own.

8. About two months later or longer if you need to, you should be experiencing seeing ghosts or spirits, either in a shadow form, an outline of a Human body or what I started seeing first was their face. Later when I got better at this I started seeing their whole body, including hair color, eye color and clothes. Seeing or feeling a spirit or ghost means you will need a ghost or spirit to practice on in order to develop this ability. When you are out and about and you feel a ghostly presence or maybe at home, concentrate on opening up your 3rd or 6th Chakra's and relax your mind and let the image come in. Here is the hard part. Trusting what you are seeing in your mind to be what the ghost/person looks like. Trusting in what you are seeing is what took me a long time to get right. I

was lucky and had Peter James to tell me what I was seeing was right or wrong. If you are lucky to know a Medium then ask them if they can assist you. If not, then you will just have to work at it alone and trust your instinct that what you are seeing is real. Practice opening up and seeing the ghost or spirit only for a minute or two. Not too long because we are getting used to doing this by easing into it. Each time you do this technique concentrate on the persons face first. Do this as much as possible for the next six months. Remember, close down your Chakra when you are finished. Over time (several years) I have been able to see ghosts or spirits as second nature. It is easy for me and only takes me a few seconds to see them come through. One thing I want to mention is hearing them.

Ghosts are not to be trusted. They were bad people on this Earth before they died and will lie to you in order to get in your good graces. Then they will manipulate you into doing things you may not want to do. If it is a spirit, like a relative you recognize, then you can trust them. But only you can make that determination. Always be leery of who you see and what they are telling you. Finally, when you reach this point having achieved the ability to open and close your Chakra's comfortably, you will be able to see or hear ghosts or spirits when YOU want to. Congratulations!

CHAPTER 5

NIRVANA

I thought I would touch on this subject for while it is difficult to explain, it is not impossible to obtain. Nirvana will take a lot of patience and time to achieve but if you really want it, then by all means go for it. Meditation is the only way to get there, as well as a desire to learn how to do it. It took me over two years to achieve this, so once again a lot of patience will be needed. I am sure that you have noticed that time seems to go by without you noticing when you meditate. You probably have noticed that you start meditating at the top of the hour, then when you come out of it, a lot time has passed without you even knowing it. This is true when in the Nirvana state. Being in Nirvana is when your conscious mind leaves your body and it is free from any Earthly connection. It is a state of mind where you are in a place of pure relaxation and time has no relevance. You neither feel nor hear anything when you are there.

Try this other method when you meditate or you can still use the other one I mentioned. When you are in your meditative state, concentrate on a green grassy pasture. Imagine yourself standing in the middle of it and slowly began walking. See yourself walking over a small grassy hill until you reach the top. At the top visualize looking at the ocean and hearing the waves. Just stand there and concentrate on the sound of the waves, feeling a light breeze blowing on you. Thinking, seeing and hearing the ocean is another one of the most relaxing and calming places that I know. It is serene. After a while your mind or spirit guide will tell you that it is time to come back and you will find yourself back in your body and awake. This is the best way I can describe it, for I have been there several times and the feeling is wonderful. I seem to appreciate life a lot better and treat myself with more appreciation and respect.

CHAPTER 6

BEING IN CONTROL

At this stage you should be seeing or hearing ghosts or spirits less and less or not at all. When your Chakra energy point is open you will be able to see and possibly hear them when you want. When you close your Chakra's then you should not see or hear anything. If you do, then go back and meditate practicing opening and closing them again and again. Like I said, you will have to keep on top of your meditation skills throughout your life time. Don't get too relaxed and think just because you haven't experienced anything in a while doesn't mean that your abilities have completely shut down. Re-read this booklet and keep in practice.

I hope this booklet has given you some insight on what you are experiencing and helped you to control your abilities into a manageable way so you can enjoy life better without the distractions of ghost entities that surround us. After reading this booklet and you have questions, please feel free to e-mail me at www.paulrogers@pgrparanormal.com.

Made in the USA
San Bernardino, CA
07 May 2018